THiS BOOK BELONGS tO:

Brimming with creative inspiration, how-to projects, and useful information to enrich your everyday life, Quarto Knows is a favorite destination for those pursuing their interests and passions. Visit our site and dig deeper with our books into your area of interest: Quarto Creates, Quarto Cooks, Quarto Homes, Quarto Lives, Quarto Drives, Quarto Explores, Quarto Gifts, or Quarto Kids.

First published in French as
Dictionnaire des bonnes manières pour enfants,
Dictionnaire des grosses bêtises, and
Dictionnaire de parfair écolier.
© Larousse 2014, 2016, 2017

Published in English in 2018 by Walter Foster Jr.,
an imprint of The Quarto Group.
6 Orchard Road, Suite 100, Lake Forest, CA 92630, USA.
T (949) 380-7510 **F** (949) 380-7575 **www.QuartoKnows.com**

Walter Foster Jr. titles are also available at discount for retail, wholesale, promotional, and bulk purchase. For details, contact the Special Sales Manager by email at specialsales@quarto.com or by mail at The Quarto Group, Attn: Special Sales Manager, 401 Second Avenue North, Suite 310, Minneapolis, MN 55401 USA.

ISBN: 978-1-63322-525-1

Illustrated by Philippe Jalbert
Translated by Juliet Lecouffe

Printed in China
10 9 8 7 6 5 4 3 2 1

MIX
Paper from
responsible sources
FSC® C104723

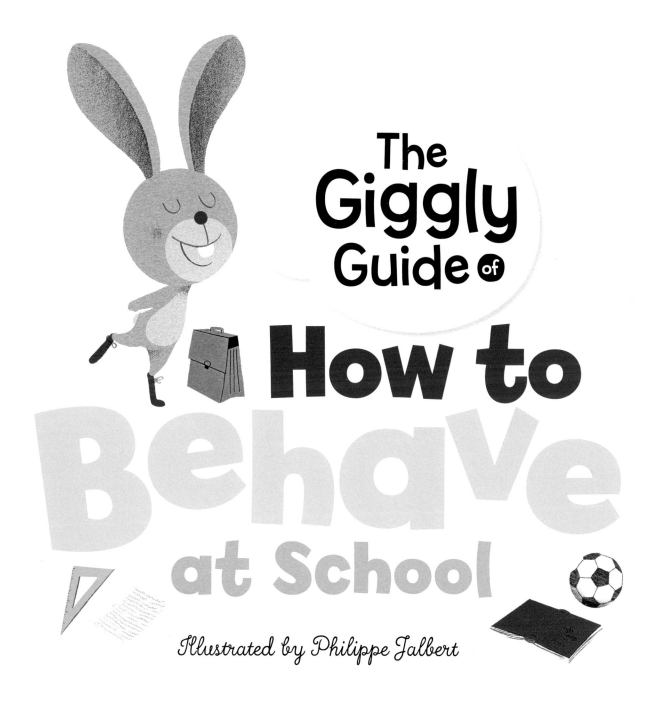

The Giggly Guide of How to Behave at School

Illustrated by Philippe Jalbert

The perfect student is always dressed appropriately.

It's not nice to
make fun of others,
even if they are
a little different.

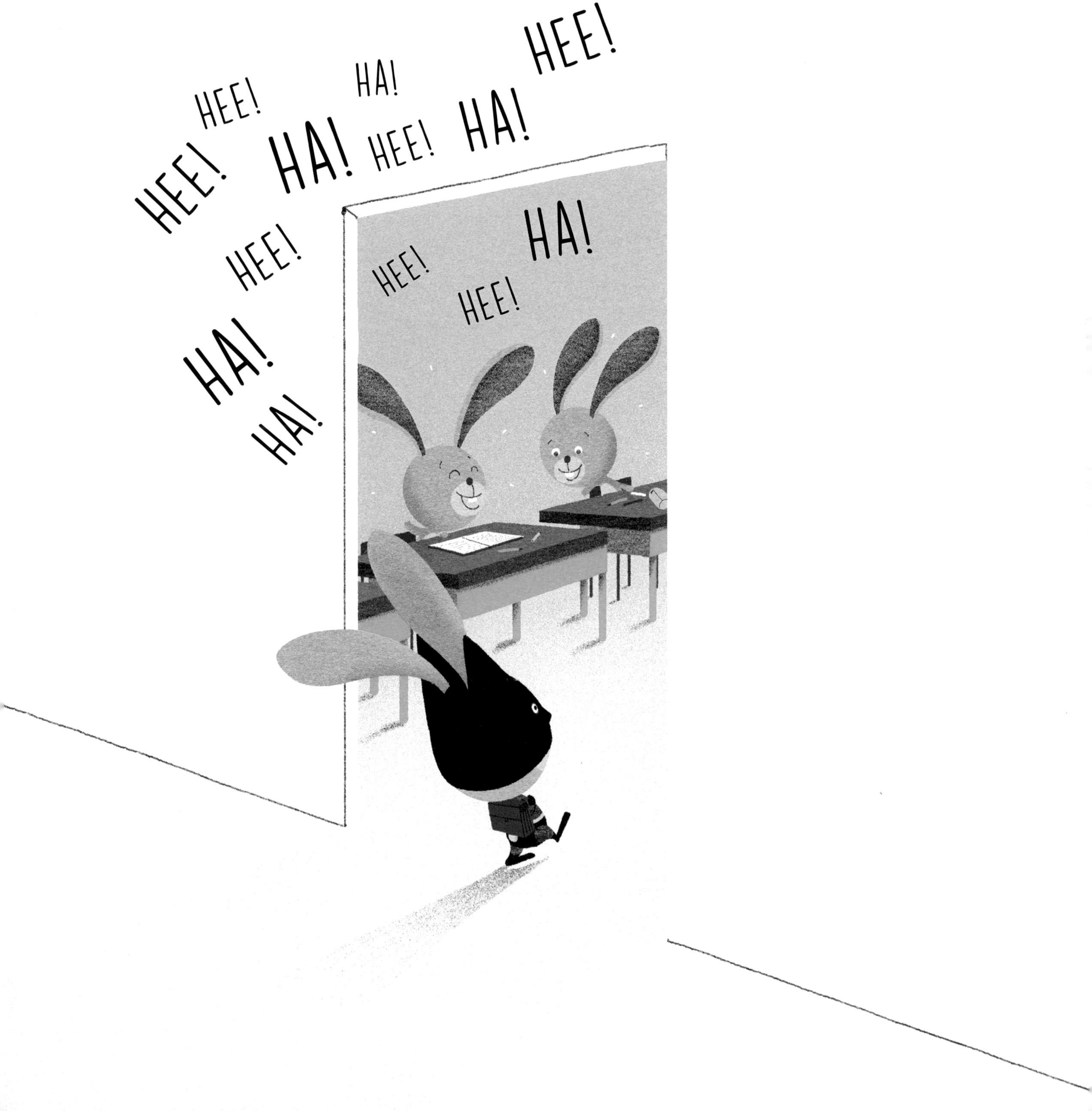
HEE!
HA!
HEE!
HA!
HEE!
HA!
HEE!
HA!
HEE!
HEE!
HEE!
HA!
HA!

It's good to get creative—
just not with your
school supplies.

When the bell rings, walk (don't run!) in the halls or down the stairs.

Chewing gum in class is a bad idea.

Always give your best effort, even if it takes a little longer.

It's important to pay attention in class.

Be careful not to press too hard with your pencil.

Always sit properly in your chair.

On school trips, stay with your assigned partner.

Try not to make a
mess when painting.

If you spill something, clean it up.

Don't borrow things from the classroom without permission.

And only bring what
you need to school.

Lunchtime is
for eating, not for
playing with your food.

It's not polite to place your elbows on the table when you eat.

After lunch, be sure to wash your hands before going back to class.

When you want to speak up in class, raise your hand and wait to be called.

Pay attention and listen when others are talking.

It's always best to use the restroom before class begins.

Be sure to hang
up your backpack
properly.

It's good manners to respect your classmates' personal space.

It's best to
keep your hands
to yourself.

When it comes to
expressing your
creativity, keep it on
paper or the board.

It's not a good idea to play with the teacher's things—even if it's in the name of love.

Be sure to take off your hat before entering the classroom.

If you have a
problem, ask an
adult for help.

The perfect student is curious—but not about everything.

Don't play in
the restroom.

Always wash and
dry your hands after
using the restroom.

Screaming at school never turns out well.

Your desk should always
be neat and tidy.

The perfect student is always on time.

Don't be afraid of making new friends. Just smile and say "Hello!"

Listening to others' conversations is not polite.

Be sure to open and close classroom doors carefully.

Always watch where you are walking.

Books are for reading,
not for crafting.

At the library, put books back on the shelf when you're done with them.

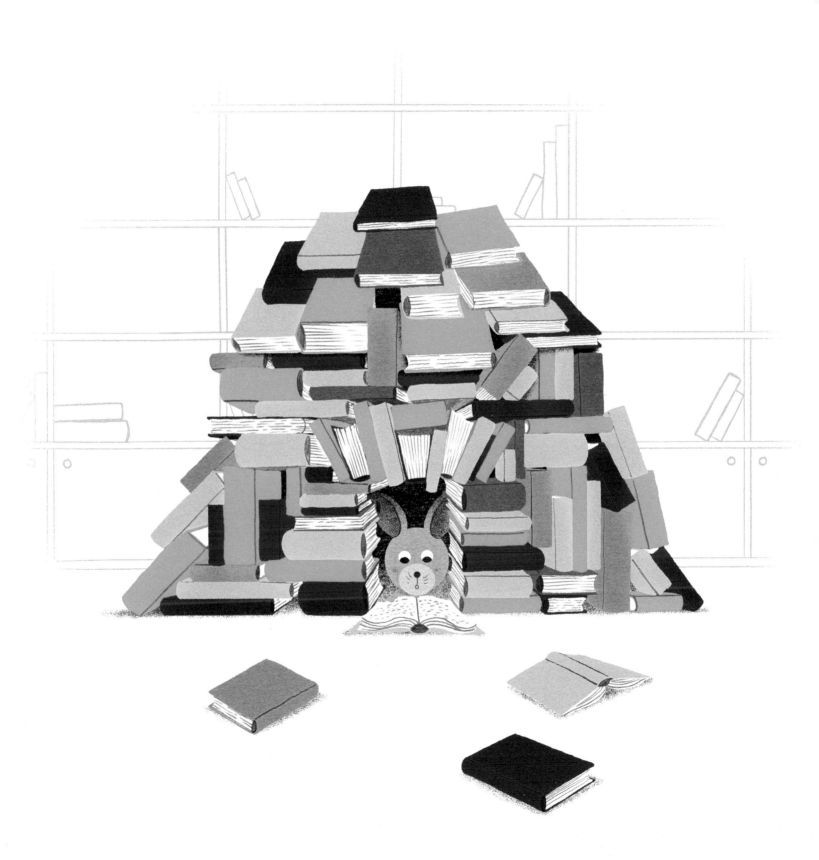

If you need to reach something on the top shelf, ask for help.

It's not okay to copy someone else's work.

Even if you're excited to get home after school, be sure to look where you're going.

During nap time,
don't make noise
while others
are sleeping.

Always be polite
at school, and
everywhere you go.